First published in Great Britain in 1997 by
BROCKHAMPTON PRESS
20 Bloomsbury Street, London WC1B 3QA
a member of the Hodder Headline Group

© Brockhampton Press, 1997
© Mari Friend (all illustrations), 1997
© Savitri Books (text compilation), 1997

ISBN 1-86019-411-7

Printed and bound in Italy

PROSE & VERSE
IN PRAISE OF

NATURE

Illustrated by Mari Friend

BROCKHAMPTON PRESS

… amongst the beautiful green grass grew a little daisy. The sun shone as warmly and as brightly upon it as on the great splendid garden flowers, and so it grew from hour to hour. One morning it stood in full bloom, with its little shining white petals spreading like rays round the little yellow sun in the centre. It never thought that no man would notice it down in the grass, and that it was a poor despised little flower; no, it was very merry, and turned to the warm sun, looked up to it, and listened to the lark carolling high in the air.

Hans Christian Andersen, *The Daisy*

Spring, the sweet spring, is the year's pleasant king;
Then blooms each thing, then maids dance in a ring,
Cold doth not sting, the pretty birds do sing:
   Cuckoo, jug-jug, pu-we, to-witta-woo!

Thomas Nashe, *Spring*

What a great pleasure and delight there is in being really sentimental. I thought about this as I picked flowers in the garden this morning – violets – a great patch of them smelling lovely, sweeter than the lids of Juno's eyes, primroses plain and coloured, scyllas and wild celandines, so very much spring flowers. People who are not sentimental, who never keep relics, brood on anniversaries, kiss photographs good-night and good-morning, must miss a good deal.

Barbara Pym, *A Very Private Eye*

All Nature seems at work, Slugs leave their lair –
The bees are stirring – birds are on the wing –
And Winter, slumbering in the open air,
Wears on his smiling face a dream of Spring!

Samuel Taylor Coleridge, *Work without Hope*

From the time of the arrival of the first
swallow the flowers take heart; the few and
scanty plants that had braved the earlier cold
are succeeded by a constantly enlarging list,
till the banks and lanes are full of them.

Richard Jefferies, *Nature on the Roof*

The woods were awe-inspiringly quiet. Even the children hushed their sing-song chatter as they scuffled along in the beech leaves. Signs of spring were everywhere. The honeysuckle is already in small leaf, the primrose plants are sturdy rosettes, and we saw several birds with dry grass or feathers in beak, and a speculative glint in the eye.

'Miss Read', *Village Diary*

Snowdrops quite out, but cold & winterly – yet for all this a thrush that lives in our orchard has shouted & sung its merriest all day long.

Dorothy Wordsworth, *Grasmere Journal*

I never saw daffodils so beautiful...they grew among the mossy stones about & about them, some rested their heads upon these stones as on a pillow for weariness & the rest tossed & reeled & danced & seemed as if they verily laughed with the wind that blew them over the Lake, they looked so gay ever glancing ever changing.

Dorothy Wordsworth, *Grasmere Journal*

The wood rich in flowers; a beautiful yellow,
palish yellow, flower, that looked thick, round,
and double, and smelt very sweet – I supposed it was
a ranunculus. Crowfoot, the grassy-leaved rabbit-
toothed white flower, strawberries, geranium,
scentless violets, anemones two kinds,
orchises, primroses.

Dorothy Wordsworth, *Grasmere Journal*

The air is precious to the red man, for all things share
the same breath – the beast, the tree and the human.
The white man does not seem to notice the air
he breathes.

Chief Seattle

Seldom do we realize that the world is practically no thicker to us than the print of our footsteps on the path. Upon that surface we walk and act our comedy of life, and what is underneath is nothing to us. But it is out from that under-world, from the dead and the unknown, from the cold moist ground, that these green blades have sprung.

Richard Jefferies, *Out of Doors in February*

Nothing is so beautiful as Spring –
   When weeds, in wheels, shoot long and lovely and
     lush;
   Thrush's eggs look little low heavens, and thrush
Through the echoing timber does so rinse and wring
The ear, it strikes like lightnings to hear him sing.

Gerard Manley Hopkins, *Spring*

In the Spring a livelier iris changes on the burnish'd
   dove;
In the Spring a young man's fancy lightly turns to
   thoughts of love.

Alfred, Lord Tennyson, *Locksley Hall*

There was a roaring in the wind all night;
The rain came heavily and fell in floods;
But now the sun is rising calm and bright;
The birds are singing in the distant woods.

William Wordsworth,
Resolution and Independence

When daisies pied and violets blue
    And lady-smocks all silver-white
And cuckoo-buds of yellow hue
    Do paint the meadows with delight.
The cuckoo then, on every tree,
Mocks married men; for this sings he,
Cuckoo.

William Shakespeare,
Love's Labour's Lost

The tree frills in a slight breeze which arrives suddenly like a sigh. The kestrel sways gently, eyes still on me. The nicotiana, the white and yellow daisies, the magenta bells of the fuchsia rustle and swing and suddenly, as if the breeze had been a signal, the kestrel takes off in a long low swoop, glides across the lawns, flustering the bag-ladies, planes upwards over the trees on the boundary and is lost to sight.

Dirk Bogarde, *A Short Walk from Harrods*

But it was May and the warm wind dried her eyes and soothed her sore eyelids, and the roadside banks were covered with the tiny spring flowers she loved, stitchwort and celandine and whole sheets of speedwell, which Laura knew as angel's eyes, and somewhere in the budding green hedgerow a blackbird was singing. Who could be sad on such a day!

Flora Thompson, *Lark Rise to Candleford*

And after April, when May follows,
And the whitethroat builds, and all the swallows!
Hark, where my blossomed pear-tree in the hedge
Leans to the field and scatters on the clover
Blossoms and dewdrops – at the bent spray's edge –
That's the wise thrush; he sings each song twice over,
Lest you should think he could never recapture
The first fine careless rapture!

Robert Browning,
Home Thoughts from Abroad

Sweet are the uses of adversity,
Which like the toad, ugly and venomous,
Wears yet a precious jewel in his head;
And this our life, exempt from public haunt,
Finds tongues in trees, books in the running brooks,
Sermons in stones and good in everything.

William Shakespeare, *As You Like It*

I know a little garden close
Set thick with lily and red rose,
Where I would wander if I might
From dewy dawn to dewy night,
And have one with me wandering.

William Morris,
The Life and Death of Jason

What wondrous life is this I lead!
Ripe apples drop about my head;
The luscious clusters of the vine
Upon my mouth do crush their wine;
The nectarine and curious peach
Into my hands themselves do reach;
Stumbling on melons, as I pass,
Ensnared with flowers, I fall on grass.

Andrew Marvell, *The Garden*

To gild refined gold, to paint the lily,
To throw a perfume on the violet,
To smooth the ice, or add another hue
Unto the rainbow, or with taper light
To seek the beauteous eye of heaven to garnish
Is wasteful and ridiculous excess.

William Shakespeare, *King John*

And in the warm hedge grew lush eglantine,
    Green cowbind and the moonlight-coloured may,
And cherry-blossoms, and white cups, whose wine
    Was the bright dew, yet drained not by the day;
And wild roses, and ivy serpentine,
    With its dark buds and leaves, wandering astray;
And flowers azure, black, and streaked with gold,
    Fairer than any wakened eyes behold.

Percy Bysshe Shelley, *The Question*

And in my breast
Spring wakens too; and my regret
　Becomes an April violet
　And buds and blossoms like the rest.

Alfred, Lord Tennyson,
In Memoriam

How sweet I roamed from field to field,
　And tasted all the summer's pride,
Till I the prince of love beheld,
　Who in the sunny beams did glide!

He showed me lilies for my hair,
　And blushing roses for my brow;
He led me through his gardens fair,
　Where all his golden pleasures grow.

William Blake, *Song*

The cuckoo is a merry bird,
He sings as he flies,
He brings us glad tidings
And tells us no lies.

Trad, *The Cuckoo*

And the jessamine faint, and the sweet tuberose,
The sweetest flower for scent that blows.

Percy Bysshe Shelley, *The Sensitive Plant*

Oh! there the chestnuts, summer through,
Beside the river make for you
A tunnel of green gloom, and sleep
Deeply above …

Here tulips bloom as they are told;
Unkempt about those hedges blows
    An English unofficial rose.

Rupert Brooke,
The Old Vicarage, Grantchester

Dance, yellows and whites and reds, -
Lead your gay orgy, leaves, stalks, heads,
Astir with the wind in the tulip-beds!

There's sunshine; scarcely a wind at all
Disturbs starved grass and daisies small
On a certain mound by a churchyard wall.

Daisies and grass be my heart's bedfellows
On the mound wind spares and sunshine mellows:
Dance, you reds and whites and yellows!

Robert Browning, *Spring Song*

Full many a glorious morning have I seen
Flatter the mountain-tops with sovereign eye,
Kissing with golden face the meadows green,
Gliding pale streams with heavenly alchemy.

William Shakespeare, *Sonnet 33*

A few steps on and I came upon as pretty a little
scene in bird life as one could wish for: twenty to
twenty-five small birds of different species – tits,
wrens, dunnocks, thrushes, blackbirds, chaffinches,
yellowhammers – were congregated on the lower
outside twigs of a bramble bush and on the bare
ground beside it close to the foot of the wall.
The sun shone full on that spot, and they
had met for warmth and for company.

W H Hudson, *Afoot in England*

Spring had begun as at a starter's pistol. Bird song had broken out in a frenzy, a fever of building had set in, and, overnight, swallows and swifts were skimming everywhere. Martins were setting their old quarters to rights, lizards flickered on the stones, nests multiplied in the reeds, shoals teemed and the frogs, diving underwater at a stranger's approach, soon surfaced again, sounding as though they were reinforced every hour by a thousand new voices; they kept the heronries empty as long as daylight lasted. The herons themselves glided low and waded through the flagleaves with a jerky and purposeful gait, or, vigilantly on one leg like the storks, posed with cunning as plants.

Patrick Leigh Fermor,
Between the Woods and the Water

Many a flower have I seen blossom,
  Many a bird for me will sing.
Never heard I so sweet a singer,
  Never saw I so fair a thing.

She is a bird, a bird that blossoms,
  She is a flower, a flower that sings;
And I a flower when I behold her,
  And when I hear her, I have wings.

Mary Elizabeth Coleridge,
Gibberish

I know the way she went
Home with her maiden posy,
For her feet have touch'd the meadows
And left the daisies rosy.

Alfred, Lord Tennyson, *Maud*

Spring goeth all in white,
Crowned with milk-white may:
In fleecy flocks of light
O'er heaven the white clouds stray:

White butterflies in the air;
White daisies prank the ground:
The cherry and hoary pear
Scatter their snow around.

Robert Bridges,
Spring Goeth All in White

The exceeding beauty of the earth, in her splendour of life, yields a new thought with every petal. The hours when the mind is absorbed by beauty are the only hours when we really live, so that the longer we can stay among these things so much the more is snatched from inevitable Time.

Richard Jefferies, *The Pageant of Summer*

It was full Spring down there in Cornwall, and I noticed the dramatic alternations of slashing rain and sunshine, the tattered sails of cloud, the green fury of the sea, the gorse along the cliff walks and the cushions of primroses in the deep lanes, but it all seemed to be happening a long way off and to have nothing to do with me.

J B Priestley,
Bright Day

Go down to Kew in lilac-time, in lilac-time, in lilac-time;
　　Go down to Kew in lilac-time (it isn't far from London!)
And you shall wander hand in hand with love in summer's wonderland;
　　Go down to Kew in lilac-time (it isn't far from London!)

Alfred Noyes, *Barrel Organ*

Gives not the hawthorn bush a sweeter shade
To shepherds, looking on their silly sheep,
Than doth a rich embroider'd canopy
To kings that fear their subjects' treachery?

William Shakespeare,
King Henry VI Part III

The first bird I searched for was the nightjar, which used to nest in the valley. Its song is like the sound of a stream of wine spilling from a height into a deep and booming cask … If a song could smell, this song would smell of crushed grapes and almonds and dark wood. The sound spills out, and none of it is lost. The whole wood brims with it. Then it stops. Suddenly, unexpectedly. But the ear hears it still, a prolonged and fading echo, draining and winding out among the surrounding trees.

J A Baker, *The Peregrine*

Where the bee sucks, there suck I,
In a cowslip's bell I lie,
There I couch when owls do cry,
On the bat's back I do fly
After summer merrily.
   Merrily, merrily, shall I live now
   Under the blossom that hangs on the bough.

William Shakespeare, *The Tempest*

I'd be a butterfly born in a bower
Where roses and lilies and violets meet.

Thomas Haynes Bayly, *I'd Be a Butterfly*

I have been here before
　　But when or how I cannot tell:
I know the gras beyond the door,
　　The sweet keen smell,
The sighing sound, the lights around the shore.

Dante Gabriel Rossetti,
Sudden Light

The sweetest softest silent night. Clouds to the West
of a gleaming red. We leaned over the gate, admiring
the solemnity of the scene and the profound Silence
which reigned around as if we were the only
inhabitants of this sweet Valley.

Lady Eleanor Butler, *Diary*

When June is come, then all the day
I'll sit with my love in the scented hay:
And watch the sunshot palaces high,
That the white clouds build in the breezy sky.

Robert Bridges,
When June Is Come

As when, upon a tranced summer night,
Those green-rob'd senators of mighty woods,
Tall oaks, branch-charmed by the earnest stars,
Dream, and so dream all night without a stir.

John Keats, *Hyperion*

I know a bank whereon the wild thyme blows,
Where oxlips and the nodding violet grows
Quite over-canopied with luscious woodbine,
With sweet musk-roses and with eglantine.

William Shakespeare,
A Midsummer Night's Dream

The modest rose puts forth a thorn,
The humble sheep a threat'ning horn;
While the lily white shall in love delight,
Nor a thorn nor a threat stain her beauty bright.

William Blake, *The Lily*

Gather gladness from the skies;
Take a lesson from the ground;
Flowers do ope their heavenward eyes
And a Spring-time joy have found;
Earth throws Winter's robes away,
Decks herself for Easter Day.

Gerard Manley Hopkins, *Easter*

My heart leaps up when I behold
A rainbow in the sky.

William Wordsworth,
My Heart Leaps Up

And a bird overhead sang *Follow*,
And a bird to the right sang *Here*;
And the arch of the leaves was hollow,
And the meaning of May was clear.

Algernon Swinburne,
An Interlude

To you the earth yields her fruit; and you shall not
want if you but know how to fill your hands.

It is in exchanging the gifts of the earth that you
shall find abundance and be satisfied.

Yet unless the exchange be in love and kindly
justice it will but lead some to greed and others to hunger.

Kahlil Gibran, *The Prophet*

When stars are in the quiet skies,
    Then most I pine for thee;
Bend on me, then, thy tender eyes,
    As stars look on the sea!

Edward George Bulwer-Lytton,
Baron Lytton, *Ernest Maltravers*

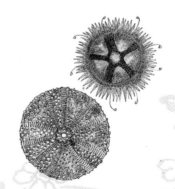

All things bright and beautiful,
    All creatures great and small,
All things wise and wonderful,
    The Lord God made them all …

The cold wind in the winter,
    The pleasant summer sun,
The ripe fruits in the garden,
    He made them every one.

Cecil Frances Alexander,
All Things Bright and Beautiful

The hundred perfumes of the little flower-garden beneath scented the air around; the deep-green meadows shone in the morning dew that glistened on every leaf as it trembled in the gentle air; and the birds sang as if every sparkling drop were a fountain of inspiration to them.

Charles Dickens, *The Pickwick Papers*

Shall I compare thee to a summer's day?
  Thou are more lovely and more temperate:
Rough winds do shake the darling buds of May,
  And summer's lease has all too short a date.
Sometime too hot the eye of heaven shines,
  And often is his gold complexion dimmed;
And every fair from fair sometimes declines,
  By chance, or nature's changing course
          untrimmed.

William Shakespeare, *Sonnet 18*

I remember, I remember,
The roses, red and white,
The vi'lets and the lily-cups,
Those flowers made of light!
The lilacs where the robin built,
And where my brother set
The laburnum on his birthday –
The tree is living yet!

Thomas Hood, *I Remember*

Art thou the bird whom man loves best,
The pious bird with the scarlet breast,
Our little English robin?

William Wordsworth,
The Redbreast Chasing the Butterfly

Come the oak before the ash,
My lady's sure to wear her sash;
Come the ash before the oak,
My lady's sure to wear her cloak.

Anon

If bees stay at home,
The rain will soon come;
If bees fly away,
It'll be a fine day.

Anon

What is pink? A rose is pink
By the fountain's brink.
What is red? A poppy's red
In its barley bed.
What is blue? The sky is blue
Where the clouds float through.
What is white? A swan is white
Sailing in the light.
What is yellow? Pears are yellow,
Rich and ripe and mellow.

What is green? The grass is green,
With small flowers between.
What is violet? Clouds are violet
In the summer twilight.
What is orange? Why, an orange,
Just an orange!

Christina Georgina Rossetti, *Sing-Song*

Stay near me – do not take thy flight!
A little longer stay in sight!
Much converse do I find in thee,
Historian of my infancy!
Float near me; do not yet depart!
Dead times revive in thee:
Thou bring'st, gay creature as thou art!
A solemn image to my heart,
My father's family!

William Wordsworth, *To a Butterfly*

And I wove the thing to a random rhyme,
For the Rose is Beauty, the Gardener, Time.

Henry Austin Dobson,
A Fancy from Fontenelle

She is the violet,
The daisy delectable,
The columbine commendable,
The jelofer amiable;
For this most goodly flower,
This blossom of fresh colour,
So Jupiter me succour,
She flourisheth new and new
In beauty and virtue.

John Skelton,
*The Commendation of
Mistress Jane Scrope*

Along the blushing borders bright with dew,
And in yon mingled wilderness of flowers,
Fair-handed Spring unbosoms every grace:
Throws out the snow-drop and the crocus first;
The daisy, primrose, violet darkly blue,
And polyanthus of unnumbered dyes;
The yellow wall-flower, stained with iron brown,
And lavish stock that scents the garden round

James Thomson, *Spring Flowers*

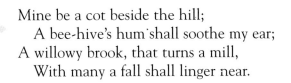

Mine be a cot beside the hill;
   A bee-hive's hum shall soothe my ear;
A willowy brook, that turns a mill,
   With many a fall shall linger near.

Samuel Rogers, *A Wish*

Within a thick and spreading hawthorn bush
That overhung a molehill large and round,
I heard from morn to morn a merry thrush
Sing hymns to sunrise, and I drank the sound
With joy; and often, an intruding guest,
I watched her secret toil from day to day.

John Clare, *The Thrush's Nest*

Summer, June summer, with the green back on earth
and the whole world unlocked and seething – like
winter, it came suddenly and one knew it in bed,
almost before waking up; with cuckoos and pigeons
hollowing the woods since daylight and the chipping
of tits in the pear-blossom.

Laurie Lee, *Cider with Rosie*

Soon will the high Midsummer pomps come on,
    Soon will the musk carnations break and swell,
Soon shall we have gold-dusted snapdragon,
Sweet-William with his homely cottage-smell,
    And stocks in fragrant blow;
Roses that down the alleys shine afar,
    And open, jasmine-muffled lattices,
    And groups under the dreaming garden-trees,
And the full moon, and the white evening star.

Matthew Arnold, *Thyrsis*

It is the harvest moon! On guilded vanes
And roofs of villages, on woodland crests
And their aerial neighbourhood of nests
Deserted, on the curtained window-panes
Of rooms where children sleep, on country lanes
And harvest fields, its mystic splendour rests!
Gone are the birds that were our summer guests,
With the last sheaves return the labouring wains!
All things are symbols: the external shows
Of nature have their image in the mind,
As flowers and fruits and falling of the leaves;
The song birds leave us at the summer's close,
Only the empty nests are left behind,
And piping of the quail among the sheaves.

H W Longfellow, *The Harvest Moon*

The water was more to me than water, the sun than sun. The gleaming rays on the water in my palm held me for a moment, the touch of the water gave me something from itself. A moment and the gleam was gone, the water flowing away, but I had had them. Beside the physical water and the physical light I had received from them their beauty; they had communicated to me this silent mystery.

Richard Jefferies, *Meadow Thoughts*

The woods extremely beautiful with all autumnal variety & softness – I carried a basket for mosses, & gathered some wild plants – Oh! that we had a book of botany – all flowers now are gay & deliciously sweet. The primrose still pre-eminent among the late flowers of the spring. Foxgloves very tall – with their heads budding.

Dorothy Wordsworth, *Grasmere Journal*

Sweet bird! thy bow'r is ever green,
 Thy sky is ever clear;
Thou hast no sorrow in thy song,
 No winter in thy year!

John Logan,
To the Cuckoo

Ethereal minstrel! pilgrim of the sky!
Dost thou despise the earth where cares abound?
Or, while the wings aspire, are heart and eye
Both with thy nest upon the dewy ground?
Thy nest which thou canst drop into at will,
Those quivering wings composed, that music still!

William Wordsworth, *To a Skylark*

The merry brown hares came leaping
Over the crest of the hill,
Where the clover and corn lay sleeping
Under the moonlight still.

Charles Kingsley, *The Bad Squire*

Throughout the summer the monarch is a common sight in the gardens and countryside of North America, but in late summer and early autumn it begins its journey south. This migration flight, from the Great Lakes in the north to Texas or the Gulf of Mexico in the south, covers between 2000 and 3000 km (1250–1850 miles). Many of the towns on the monarch's flight path have festivals or carnivals to celebrate the arrival of the butterflies. I have seen clouds of them flying southwards through Texas, with steady wing-beats. They were about 4–6 metres (15–20 feet) above the ground and travelled at about 17 km (11 miles) an hour. It was a never-to-be-forgotten sight.

Mari Friend, *Winter Survival*

Season of mists and mellow fruitfulness!
  Close bosom-friend of the maturing sun;
Conspiring with him how to load and bless
  With fruit the vines that round the thatch-eaves run;
To bend with apples the mossed cottage-trees,
  And fill all fruit with ripeness to the core;
To swell the gourd, and plump the hazel shells
With a sweet kernel; to set budding more,
And still more, later flowers for the bees.

John Keats, *To Autumn*

A glorious day, still autumnal and not wintry.
We have had a delicious walk in the Park, and I
think the colouring of the scenery is more beautiful
than ever. Many of the oaks are still thickly covered
with leaves of a rich yellow-brown; the elms, golden
sometimes, still with lingering patches of green.

George Eliot, *Diary*

It is autumn, Mariana thought. My summer has gone already. Summer, life, love seemed to be leaving her together.

One night when the maple tree above the house was growing pink and flame coloured she left the cottage and started to walk through the fields and dark woods beyond her little wood. A thin red line of sunset was still in the sky as she brushed through the golden rod in the fields, but when she entered the woods again, the thick-growing trees hid it. She could only see the clear, cold sky with the first stars beginning to shine out…

Mariana went rapidly through the woods; little as she feared wandering alone, she did not want the darkness to catch her under the trees. She found herself hurrying and laughed at her fears. There is nothing in these woods, she told herself, nothing to be afraid of.

 Gamel Woolsey, *One Way of Love*

The rainbow comes and goes,
And lovely is the rose,
Look round her when the heavens are bare,
Waters on a starry night
Are beautiful and fair;
The sunshine is a glorious birth:
But yet I know, where'er I go,
That there hath passed away a glory from the earth.

William Wordsworth, Ode,
Intimations of Immortality

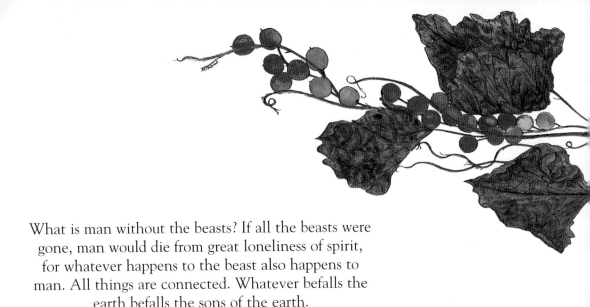

What is man without the beasts? If all the beasts were
gone, man would die from great loneliness of spirit,
for whatever happens to the beast also happens to
man. All things are connected. Whatever befalls the
earth befalls the sons of the earth.

Chief Seattle

The comeliness of autumn was imbued in the earth,
The endless blue sky was free from blemish,
A boundless white glow spread over the space,
Nature seemed to blossom with gaiety.

By the river bank in the woods and in the caves
Slowly flowed the clear springs of water,
Their incessant sound has an appeal so rare,
For they sang the glory of victorious autumn.

Ayodhya Singh Upadhyaya, *The Great Dance*

As temperatures fall, so do the leaves. For centuries, country people have watched the behaviour of trees in autumn closely and used it to predict the following winter's weather: 'October with green leaves means a severe winter' is one of many pieces of folk wisdom, most of which seem to spread gloom and despondency. I expect this is because few of us look forward to the short days, long nights and cold of the winter. But when the rich colours of summer begin to dissipate in autumn, there is a burst of splendour as green leaves change to gold, orange, russet or deep crimson. Some trees are more beautiful in autumn than at any other time of the year, their lofty crowns reminding us of the brilliant colour of captured sunsets or perhaps the flickering fires of frosty nights.

Mari Friend, *Winter Survival*

The chief features of October on the meadows were the hordes of mushrooms and toadstools that sprang up in every corner and the wealth of fruit that ripened in the hedges. These hedgerow fruits provided much of the colour, for the leaves were late in turning, and by the end of the month, although some trees, such as the large Willows, were almost bare, the majority were still green, even if splashed here and there with touches of yellow and russet … Fungus growth reached its peak during the first two weeks, which saw a combination of warm sunshine, moist soil and dewy nights. Toadstools came up everywhere … From every visit I would bring back a plastic bag full of specimens for identification, and I spent long hours at my desk sorting them out and trying, frequently without success, to name them.

Benjamin Perkins, *A Secret Landscape*

Welcome, wild North-easter!
Shame it is to see
Odes to every zephyr;
Ne'er a verse to thee.

Charles Kingsley,
Ode to the North-East Wind

The Oak is called the king of trees,
The Aspen quivers in the breeze,
The Poplar grows up straight and tall,
The Peach tree spreads along the wall,
The Sycamore gives pleasant shade,
The Willow droops in watery glade,
The Fir tree useful timber gives,
The Beech amid the forest lives.

Sara Coleridge, *Trees*

Therefore all seasons shall be sweet to thee,
Whether the summer clothe the general earth
With greenness, or the redbreast sit and sing
Betwixt the tufts of snow on the bare branch
Of mossy apple-tree, while the night thatch
Smokes in the sun-thaw; whether the eaves-drops fall
Heard only in the trances of the blast,
Or in the secret ministry of frost
Shall hang them up in silent icicles,
Quietly shining to the quiet moon.

Samuel Taylor Coleridge, *Frost at Midnight*

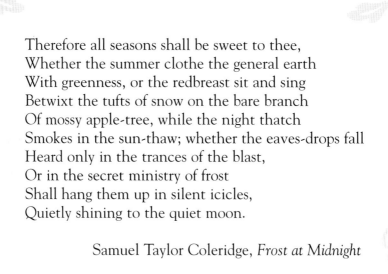

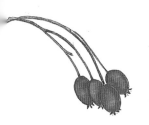

The last leaves measure our years; they are gone as the days are gone, and the bare branches silently speak of a new year, slowly advancing to its buds, its foliage and fruit.

Richard Jefferies, *January in the Sussex Woods*

Winter has arrived at last, and with a vengeance. The first flurries of snow, which left a fine powdering on the ground, arrived a few days ago, and today as I walked over the meadow there was an inch of snow on the ground and more falling, fine at first but turning to large flakes by the time I left.

Benjamin Perkins, *A Secret Landscape*

I walked abroad in a snowy day;
I asked the soft snow with me to play.
She played and she melted all in her prime,
And the winter called it a dreadful crime.

William Blake, *Soft Snow*

An owl that in a barn
Sees a mouse creeping in the corn,
Sits still and shuts his round blue eyes,
As if he slept, until he spies
The little beast within his reach
Then starts, and seizes on the wretch.

Samuel Butler, *Hudibras*

The south wind always brings wet weather,
The north wind wet and cold together.
The west wind always brings the rain,
And the east wind blows it back again.

Traditional verse

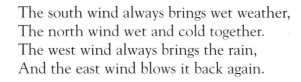

The day is done, and the darkness
Falls from the wings of Night,
As a feather is wafted downward
From an eagle in his flight.

Henry Wadsworth Longfellow,
The Day is Done

Holly is a welcome source of brightness in this
otherwise rather colourless season. So, too, was this
morning's hoar frost, which painted the meadows
sparkling white.

Benjamin Perkins, *A Secret Landscape*

The holly and the ivy,
When they are both full grown,
Of all the trees that are in the wood
the holly bears the crown

Anon,

The fountains mingle with the river,
    And the rivers with the ocean;
The winds of heaven mix for ever
    With a sweet emotion;
Nothing in the world is single;
    All things, by a law divine,
In one another's being mingle.
    Why not I with thine?

Percy Bysshe Shelley,
Love's Philosophy

November 13th 1776. Nuthatches rap about on the
trees. Crocus begin to sprout. The leaves of the
medlar-tree are now turned of a bright yellow. One of
the first trees that becomes naked is the walnut; the
mulberry, and the ash, especially if it bears many
keys, and the horse-chestnut comes next.

Gilbert White,
Natural History and Antiquities of Selborne

It sifts from leaden sieves,
It powders all the wood,
It fills with alabaster wool
The wrinkles of the road.

It makes an even face
Of mountain and of plain,
Unbroken forehead from the east
Unto the east again.

Emily Dickinson,
The Snow

Badgers give birth to their young following a period of prolonged inactivity in winter. In Britain, this usually occurs during January or early February: it may be a little earlier in the south, while in the north and east it may be a little later. Up to five youngsters are born; they are blind and helpless and they snuggle together in the deep bed of straw, hay, bracken and dead leaves which makes up their cosy nest. It is important that the nursery chamber in the badgers' sett is well furnished with large quantities of insulating material, as this helps the cubs to retain their body heat, particularly when their mother has left them alone while she forages for food to maintain her own strength and keep up her milk supply.

Mari Friend, *Winter Survival*